30118128224866

The Goose
that laid the
Golden Eggs

Retold by Mairi Mackinnon

Illustrated by
Daniel Howarth

Reading Consultant: Alison Kelly
Roehampton University

This story is about

Tom,

Elena,

a little white
goose,

2

a goat,

some hens

and
a goldsmith.

3

This map shows where
Tom and Elena live.

Hills

Tom and Elena's
cottage

The hen
shed

Road to the
village

The village

The goldsmith

The market

Tom lived in a small cottage...

with his wife Elena.

They were very poor

but they had everything
they needed.

They had a goat to give
them milk.

They had a garden to grow vegetables

and they had hens and
geese for fresh eggs.

Every morning, Tom collected the eggs.

He took them to sell
in the village.

One morning he found
something strange.

One of the eggs was dark
yellow and very heavy.

At first Tom thought it
was a trick.

Elena was amazed.

That's not a stone, Tom!

It was a solid golden egg.

Tom took all the eggs
to the village.

Then he went to see
the goldsmith.

The goldsmith was
amazed too. He wanted
to buy the egg.

How much?

Tom had never seen so much money.

He bought a new dress
for Elena.

Then he went home.

That evening, Tom gave Elena her new dress. She wasn't happy.

Tom thought. Maybe
Elena was right. Maybe
he should have saved
the money.

But it was too late. He
had spent all of it.

27

Then, the next morning, he found another golden egg.

Now we can fix the roof.

And the next morning he found another.

Every day Tom sold a
golden egg.

He bought new clothes
for himself and Elena.

He built a bigger
and better house.

They had a big garden
and lots of servants.

Tom and Elena
were rich!

But Tom wanted more.

One golden egg a day
wasn't enough.

He wanted lots of gold.

"Let's kill the goose," said Elena.

Then we'll have all the gold at once!

They crept outside.

Squawk!

Elena grabbed the goose.
Tom killed it.

39

Then they cut the
goose open.

But there was no gold
inside at all.

"What have we done?"
they said.

No more
gold!

We'll be poor
again!

They had been
too greedy. Now they
had lost everything.

Tom collected the
eggs every morning.
He never found
another golden egg.

About this story

"The Goose that laid the Golden Eggs" is one of Aesop*'s Fables. These are a collection of short stories first told in Ancient Greece around 4,000 years ago.

*say Ee-sop

Nobody knows exactly who Aesop was, but the stories are still popular today, and they are known all around the world.

The stories
are often about
animals, and they
always have a "moral"
(a message or lesson)
at the end.

The moral of the story
about the golden eggs is:

Don't be greedy or you
might lose everything.

Series editor:
Lesley Sims

Designed by
Russell Punter and Louise Flutter.

First published in 2006 by Usborne Publishing Ltd., Usborne House,
83-85 Saffron Hill, London EC1N 8RT, England. www.usborne.com
Copyright © 2006 Usborne Publishing Ltd.